OVERCOMING
the Shame in Life

DARRELL D. KELLY

Author's Tranquility Press
ATLANTA, GEORGIA

Copyright © 2024 by Darrell D. Kelly

All rights reserved. No part of this publication may be reproduced, distributed or transmitted in any form or by any means, including photocopying, recording, or other electronic or mechanical methods, without the prior written permission of the publisher, except in the case of brief quotations embodied in critical reviews and certain other noncommercial uses permitted by copyright law. For permission requests, write to the publisher, addressed "Attention: Permissions Coordinator," at the address below.

Darrell D. Kelly/Author's Tranquility Press
3900 N Commerce Dr. Suite 300 #1255
Atlanta, GA 30344, USA
www.authorstranquilitypress.com

To book a speaking engagement, please contact: darrellkelly@live.com

Ordering Information:
Quantity sales. Special discounts are available on quantity purchases by corporations, associations, and others. For details, contact the "Special Sales Department" at the address above.

Overcoming the Shame in Life/Darrell D. Kelly
Paperback: 978-1-962859-83-7
eBook: 978-1-962859-85-1

Contents

Introduction
"Over Coming the Shame in Life" i

Chapter 1
"My Mistakes, My Appearance" 1

Chapter 2
"My Problem, My Difference" 9

Chapter 3
"My Parents, My Weakness" 16

Chapter 4
"My Habit" 27

Chapter 5
"Live without fear or intimidation" 32

Chapter 6
"My Testimony" 43

Introduction

"Over Coming the Shame in Life"

When we deal with the idea of not being ashamed, it is easy in church environments, singles meetings and youth rallies. When you are around other Christians and when you are in church, it is easy to say, "I love Jesus." As Christians we are "not ashamed" or afraid to be Christians when we are with one another. How we act in front of the world and those who are not Christians often becomes a different story.

If we had an inspection right now to search all of your bags, purses, music collections, your websites saved under favorites, your stuff, and your room in general, would we find something that you would be ashamed of? Think of it this way, if for some tragic reason you died today and someone was given the task of cleaning out your room, would they find anything you would be ashamed of?

When there is something in your life that's not right, safe, decent, or Godly and the very people that you wish to hide it from actually end up finding out about it, that's when shame rises to enter into your life.

When you know someone who is involved in a situation that they shouldn't be in, shame tries to set in when the word gets out about what they are doing. Maybe it's an issue of abuse, a friend getting arrested or a girl who gets pregnant. Perhaps you are one of the ones experiencing shame and embarrassment in some area of your life. My prayer is that at some point while you are reading this book, you will understand how Jesus Christ has given you the power to overcome the shame in life.

Chapter 1

"My Mistakes, My Appearance"

<u>Luke 15:11-24</u>

11 And he said, A certain man had two sons: **12** And the younger of them said to his father, Father, give me the portion of goods that falleth to me. And he divided unto them his living. **13** And not many days after the younger son gathered all together, and took his journey into a far country, and there wasted his substance with riotous living. **14** And when he had spent all, there arose a mighty famine in that land; and he began to be in want. **15** And he went and joined himself to a citizen of that country; and he sent him into his fields to feed swine. **16** And he would fain have filled his belly with the husks that the swine did eat: and no man gave unto him. **17** And when he came to himself, he said, How many hired servants of my father's have bread enough and to spare, and I perish with hunger! **18** I will arise and go to my father, and will say unto him, Father, I have sinned against heaven, and before thee, **19** And am no more worthy to be called thy son: make me as one of thy hired servants. **20** And he arose, and came to his father. But when he was yet a great way off, his father saw him, and had compassion, and ran, and fell on his neck, and kissed him. **21** And the son said unto him, Father, I have sinned against heaven, and in thy sight, and am no more worthy to be called thy son. **22** But the father said to his servants, Bring forth the best robe, and put it on him; and put a ring on his hand, and shoes on his feet: **23** And bring hither the fatted calf, and kill it; and let us eat, and be merry: **24** For *this my son was dead, and is alive again; he was lost, and is found. And they began to be merry.*

The shame in life # 1 is: "My Mistakes." In this story, the young man really had a good life at his father's house. Soon he decides that he wants his part of the inheritance so that he can move out and go his own way. First of all, his mistake was asking his dad for his share of the inheritance while his dad is "Still Alive!" In the Hebrew culture, this was an insult to his dad. By asking for this inheritance, this boy was "Wishing his father was Dead!"

Not long after getting his inheritance, this young man travels to a foreign country and when he gets there, he begins to waste all of his money and inheritance on lavish & wasteful living. He gained friends and attention by being a showoff with his riotous living.

This young man finally got to the point where he had spent all the money he had. That's when the Bible says a famine came to that land. A famine represents a time of economic crisis. There is no production, no jobs, not much to eat, resources and supplies becomes scarce. In the worst time of this young man's life, stranded in a different country with nowhere to go, he is fortunate enough to find a stranger who gives him the job of feeding pigs.

The problem is that in the Jewish culture it is forbidden to have any dealings with pigs and swine. It was not for touching, it was not for eating, it was considered unclean and against God's law. This young man, however, has been devastating to the point that not only is he willing to work with swine, but he is also starving to the point that she desires to eat the same food the pigs are eating.

16.) And he would fain have *filled his belly with the husks that the swine did eat*: *and no man gave unto him.*

The same way that this young man had a desire to fill himself with something that was unclean, is the same way that some of you are filling your lives with things that God considers unclean. This young man was so broken down at something filthy actually looked good. Some of you have become so broken down spiritually that ungodly things are attractive to you.

Some young people actually desire to be in a gang, and to have sexually promiscuous relationships. Some young people have a desire for the world's fame and fortune. Many young people not only have a desire but have an addiction to secular music and pornography. Have you ever taken the time to look within you to find out why you may have a desire for unclean things? Ask yourself: "Why do I hunger for the unholy things?"

In verses 18 and 19 of this Bible story, the young man begins to complain to himself. He says that he is going to return home to his father to confess his sins and beg his father to at least give him a job. He loses his sense of self-worth because he feels like he has disgraced the family name. Shame makes you feel unworthy. Shame makes you feel embarrassed. Shame makes you feel inadequate.

The same way this young man found the courage to return back home to his father, is the same way you must have the courage to return to God your Father. If you will be willing to rise up from any shame you have experienced in life, I will show you in these next few verses what your father God will do for you.

20.) And he arose, and came to his father. <u>But when he was yet a great way off, his father saw him</u>, and had compassion, and ran, and fell on his neck, and kissed him.

I want to highlight in this verse the fact that this young man is on his way home when his father sees him walking in the distance. This is the same way that your father God sees you and knows where you are. Because God's love is so strong, he is always watching for you to return back to him.

20.) And he arose, and came to his father. But when he was yet a great way off, his father saw him, and <u>had compassion, and ran</u>, and fell on his neck, and kissed him.

In this same verse I am now highlighting the fact that the father had compassion and ran to his son. You must understand that your father God his compassionate and eager to reunite with you. God is not waking to punish you, kick you out, or beat you down. God is full of compassion and love you more than you. He is already running to meet you right where you are.

20.) And he arose, and came to his father. But when he was yet a great way off, his father saw him, and had compassion, and ran, and <u>fell on his neck, and kissed him</u>.

Finally for verse 20, I am highlighting the fact that the father kissed his son on the neck. A kiss, of course, it's a sign of close relationship. This means that God is not going to treat you like a stranger or an outcast just because you made some mistakes. Even though the son was ashamed to return home, the father was not ashamed to receive him home.

21.) *And the son said unto him, Father, I have sinned against heaven, and in thy sight, and* **<u>am no more worthy to be called thy son.</u>**

Notice in this verse, the young man confesses his sins and expresses how worthless and embarrassed he is. It is important for us to learn that if we will confess to Jesus Christ our sins, he is faithful and just to forgive us of our sins and to cleanse us from all unrighteousness.

22.) *But the father said to his servants,* **<u>Bring forth the best robe, and put it on him;</u>** *and put a ring on his hand, and shoes on his feet:*

The father, who represents our Lord God tells his servants to put the best robe on his son. This is a sign to show you that God will cover you with the best he has to offer. Even though you have messed up, God still wants to give you his best.

The robe that the father put on his son was a symbol of status. This speaks to the fact that even when you feel like as if you are nobody, **God has a plan to restore your status** so that you will know you are somebody of great significance. You really are a person of purpose, value and dignity. You are someone special, with honor and prestige. God sees the greatness in you that you fail sometimes to see in yourself.

22.) *But the father said to his servants, Bring forth the best robe, and put it on him;* **<u>and put a ring on his hand,</u>** *and shoes on his feet:*

Now the father has instructed his servants to put a ring on his finger. This ring that the father gives his son is a sign of lineage, heritage and legacy. This ring contains the family seal which allows him to do business and make decisions on behalf of the family. When people see this ring on his hand they will automatically know that he comes from a special family of wealth and respect.

Just like the father in this story, God desires to connect you to a supernatural legacy and heritage as one of his sons and daughters. God also wants to give you power and authority to do his kingdom business on the earth. When people see you as you progress in life, God wants everyone to know that you are his child.

22.) *But the father said to his servants, Bring forth the best robe, and put it on him; and put a ring on his hand,* **and shoes on his feet***:*

The father now says to put shoes on his feet. The apostle Paul also mentions in Ephesians chapter 6 how God is giving you the shoes of peace. God wants to secure your feet so that you don't slip. He doesn't want you to trip and stumble over the same old tricks of the evil one. David said in the book of Psalms that the steps of a good man are ordered by the Lord. Allow God to lead and guide your steps so that you would not return to the shameful things again.

Shame in Life #2

Genesis 29:16-17

16.) And Laban had two daughters: the name of the elder was Leah, and the name of the younger was Rachel.

17.) Leah was tender eyed; but Rachel was beautiful and well favored.

My shame in life #2 is: "My Appearance." Leah was tender eyed, which means that whenever you looked at Leah you couldn't really tell if she was looking back at you. Her eyes did not move in the same direction at the same time. Therefore Leah found herself in competition with Rachel because Rachel was perfectly beautiful.

Some of you experience shame and embarrassment because of some physical feature about yourself that you don't like. Maybe it's your size, hair, skin tone, or having freckles. It could be that you wear braces or glasses. Maybe your pigeon toed, bow legged, cross-eyed, or have a medical condition or a more serious handicap. Before you realize it, you will start to compare yourself to other people. You will begin to question why you are the way you are while wishing to be like someone else.

The reason that you should never compare yourself to others is because they are not perfect either. Yet we are living in a day when people will pay big money to have surgery to change the way they look, and it's all because, like Leah there is something about yourself you feel ashamed of.

Psalm 100:3

3.) *Know ye that the LORD he is God: it is* **he that hath made us,** *and not we ourselves;* **we are his people,** *and the sheep of his pasture.*

It is God who has taken the time to shape and create you. It is the Lord who has formed you and has given you life. You did not make yourself, so keep in mind that you are bought with a price that is paid in full by the blood of Jesus Christ. You are the Temple of the Holy Ghost that is wonderfully made. Don't become a slave to a false self-image. You are blessed and anointed to be who God has created you to be. Today is the day that you stop being ashamed of who God made you. Be yourself in Christ and let Christ be himself in you.

Chapter 2

"My Problem, My Difference"

Shame in Life #3

<u>Mark 5:21-42</u>

21 And when Jesus was passed over again by ship unto the other side, much people gathered unto him: and he was nigh unto the sea. **22** And, behold, there cometh one of the rulers of the synagogue, Jairus by name; and when he saw him, he fell at his feet, **23** And besought him greatly, saying, My little daughter lieth at the point of death: I pray thee, come and lay thy hands on her, that she may be healed; and she shall live. **24** And Jesus went with him; and much people followed him, and thronged him. **25** And a certain woman, which had an issue of blood twelve years, **26** And had suffered many things of many physicians, and had spent all that she had, and was nothing bettered, but rather grew worse, **27** When she had heard of Jesus, came in the press behind, and touched his garment. **28** For she said, if I may touch but his clothes, I shall be whole. **29** And straightway the fountain of her blood was dried up; and she felt in her body that she was healed of that plague. **30** And Jesus, immediately knowing in himself that virtue had gone out of him, turned him about in the press, and said, Who touched my clothes? **31** And his disciples said unto him, Thou seest the multitude thronging thee, and sayest thou, Who touched me? **32** And he looked round about to see her that had done this thing. **33** But the woman fearing and trembling, knowing what was done in her, came and fell down before him, and told him all the truth. **34** And he said unto her, Daughter, thy faith hath made thee whole; go in peace, and be whole of thy plague. **35** While he yet spake, there came from the ruler of the synagogue's house certain which said, thy daughter is dead: why troublest, thou the Master any further? **36** As soon as Jesus heard the word that was spoken, he saith unto the ruler of the synagogue, Be not afraid, only believe. **37** And he suffered no man to follow him, save Peter, and James, and John the brother of James. **38** And he cometh to the house of the ruler of the synagogue, and seeth the tumult, and them that wept and wailed greatly. **39** And when he was come in, he saith unto them, Why make ye this ado, and weep? The damsel is not dead, but sleepeth. **40** And they laughed him to scorn. But when he had put them all out, he taketh the father and the mother of the damsel, and them that were with him, and entereth in where the damsel was lying. **41** And he took the damsel by the hand, and said unto her, Talitha cumi; which is, being interpreted, Damsel, I say unto thee, arise. **42** And straightway the damsel arose, and walked; for she was of the age of twelve years. And they were astonished with a great astonishment.

My shame in life #3 is: "My Problem." In this story there is a man named Jairus who has come to ask Jesus to heal his daughter because she is about to die. Jesus decides to go to this man's house to honor his request and heal his daughter.

While Jesus is on his way to Jairus' house he is interrupted by a woman with an issue of the blood. Jesus stops to make time to minister to this woman. Right then, as Jesus finished ministering to this woman, a friend of Jairus finds him and says: "do not bother Jesus anymore because your daughter has died." Jesus hearing these words turns to Jairus and tells him not to worry but continue to believe.

In verses 38 and 39 we see that Jesus has now arrived at Jairus' house. He sees all of the family members, friends, and visitors that have gathered at the house crying and weeping over the dead girl. Jesus said, "the girl is not dead, she is only asleep, so why do you make such a big deal about this?"

It is very important to notice that the people said the girl is <u>dead</u>, but Jesus is saying she is <u>only sleeping</u>. The people put this girl in the category of not being alive, but Jesus put her in the category of not being awake. Sometimes people will say that you have a problem but Jesus says that he can wake you up out of it. A counselor may put you in the category of having a disorder, but Jesus can wake you up out of it. Professionals may say that you have a condition, illness, or sickness, but Jesus still has the power to wake you up from all these things.

You do not have to live your life depressed because of some diagnosis. You can have a healthy, victorious, and abundant life in Jesus Christ. You don't have to live in depression and you don't have to kill yourself.

40.) *And they laughed him to scorn.* But when he had put them all out, *he taketh the father and the mother of the damsel, and them that were with him, and entereth in where the damsel was lying.*

When Jesus said that the girl was asleep the same people who were crying, then started laughing at him. This Scripture speaks to the fact that some people really don't want to see you rise up. Some people are laughing at the idea that you can overcome your problems. In this verse we also see that Jesus took everyone who was laughing and made them leave the house. This speaks to the fact that God is going to protect you from people who do not believe that you can rise up and make it. If you are not careful you will try to live your life in a place that is a "Dead End" or an environment where no one expects you to rise!

41.) *And he took the damsel by the hand, and said unto her, Talitha cumi; which is, being interpreted, Damsel,* ***I say unto thee, arise.***

Don't be defeated by disorders, conditions, or problems. Let Jesus take you by the hand so that he can help you rise.

42.) *And straightway the damsel arose, and walked; for she was of the age of twelve years. And they were astonished with a great astonishment.*

This verse tells us that the girl was 12 years old and the people were greatly astonished. This means that you can still be young and live the kind of life that amazes people. Make the decision today to stop living your life with all the problems that the world says you should have, and start living in all of the blessings that God says you have.

Shame in Life #4

<u>Jeremiah 1:4-10</u>

4 Then the word of the LORD came unto me, saying, 5 Before I formed thee in the belly I knew thee; and before thou came forth out of the womb I sanctified thee, and I ordained thee a prophet unto the nations. 6 Then said I, Ah, Lord GOD! behold, I cannot speak: for I am a child. 7 But the LORD said unto me, Say not, I am a child: for thou shalt go to all that I shall send thee, and whatsoever I command thee thou shalt speak. 8 Be not afraid of their faces: for I am with thee to deliver thee, saith the LORD. 9 Then the LORD put forth his hand, and touched my mouth. And the LORD said unto me, Behold, I have put my words in thy mouth. 10 See, I have this day set thee over the nations and over the kingdoms, to root out, and to pull down, and to destroy, and to throw down, to build, and to plant.

My shame in life #4 is: "My Difference." In verse 5 God begins to say that He formed you before you were even conceived in your mother's womb. God continues to say in this verse that you are sanctified and ordained. This means that before God allowed you to come into this world he already made you to be different.

Being different becomes a challenge because the world around you pressures you to fit in. It could be in school, it could be on a job, or it can be in your neighborhood, don't waste time trying to fit in when God has created you to be different.

If you fail to understand this point you will end up spending your life in the wrong places and with the wrong people. Listen, I didn't say that you would necessarily be with "bad" people, but you will end up with the "wrong" people.

To this point, many of you are so desperate to fit in that you make friendships with people who delay your progress in life. You must understand that God has placed something in your life that makes you different.

You can't help but be different when you understand that God is the one who formed you, He knows you, He sanctifies you, and He ordains you. This difference that God places in your life means that there are things in life that you just can't do.

This difference tells you that you don't need to be dating right now. This difference tells you which extracurricular activities to abstain from. This difference doesn't want you to make your life busy with just doing stuff. Sometimes when we are pursuing God, we will have to sacrifice some things that we like and things we are good at doing. This difference shows you that it's more important to do what God wants you to do that for you to do what you want to do.

6.) Then said I, Ah, Lord GOD! behold, *I cannot speak: for I am a child.*

7.) But the LORD said unto me, Say not, I am a child: *for thou shalt go to all that I shall send thee, and whatsoever I command thee thou shalt speak.*

Jeremiah says that he is unable to speak because he is a child. He began to feel as if his difference made him unable to do God's will. But the Lord is saying: "don't tell me what you can't do." God already created you to be a leader. You are not too young to be a minister. You are not too young to move in the power of God. You are not too young to have wisdom. You are not too young to operate in the anointing. This difference in your life is the reason why you cannot have premarital sex, or smoke and drink, or get tattoos and body piercings, your body is the temple of God, and it is your responsibility to keep it pure. This difference changes your wardrobe and your dress code causing you to realize that it is not appropriate to show your underwear, or your boobs. Follow the faith and not the fashions. God doesn't need Christians who have confused self-images, such as divas, hustlers, and thugs; but he needs you to be set apart from the world for his glory.

Chapter 3

"My Parents, My Weakness"

Shame in Life #5

<u>Zechariah 1:1-5</u>

1 In the eighth month, in the second year of Darius, came the word of the LORD unto Zechariah, the son of Berechiah, the son of Iddo the prophet, saying, 2 The LORD hath been sore displeased with your fathers. 3 Therefore say thou unto them, Thus saith the LORD of hosts; Turn ye unto me, saith the LORD of hosts, and I will turn unto you, saith the LORD of hosts. 4 Be ye not as your fathers, unto whom the former prophets have cried, saying, Thus saith the LORD of hosts; Turn ye now from your evil ways, and from your evil doings: but they did not hear, nor hearken unto me, saith the LORD. 5 Your fathers, where are they? And the prophets, do they live forever?

My shame in life #5 is: "My Parents." In verse two God is telling the prophet that he is extremely displeased with the fathers. The message to young people in verse 3 is to turn to God and God will turn to you. God is displeased with the parents because they would not listen to his instructions or follow his word. The reason why some of your families are divided is because there are parents who failed to obey God's word.

I have seen many Christian young people who really do have "crazy" parents. Some have unsaved parents. Some are abusive and many parents are absent. Some parents are alcoholics, and some parents are workaholics. It's not uncommon for parents who are divorced to also cause shame and embarrassment in the lives of their children.

As young people it is important for you to realize that **you are not responsible for your parents' choices and actions.** Even if you have been made to feel the blame and shame, it really isn't your fault that your parents have failed to do their job. God is in fact displeased with every parent who has not been a godly parent. In every generation God sends people to give good advice and instructions. Sometimes children make excuses for their parents, and try to block it out of their mind. Then there are those parents who really didn't know better but honestly did the best that they could. Your parents already know that they should have and could have done better. Their biggest mistake was not paying attention to the word of God.

The breakdown of a family often results in feelings of regret, bitterness, anger, and not being forgiving. These family issues are truly hard to overcome. God, however, is calling for you to turn to him in the midst of family distress. Sometimes we don't know who we can turn to. Sometimes we don't know who to call, or who we can trust. That is why I am glad that God calls us to turn and depend on Him. Don't waste time hating your parents. God is a God of peace, healing, security, and rest. God is able to fix your broken heart, your broken dreams, and your broken spirit. It is God who will give you purpose, significance, confidence and the power to move forward in life. God loves you even if you can't feel what love is. God loves you even when you feel like he is not concerned about your life.

The worst thing you could do is repeat the same mistake as your parents, and that is ignoring the word of God. It is vital that you don't turn away from God.

2 Corinthians 6:16-18

16.) *And what agreement hath the temple of God with idols? For ye are the temple of the living God; as God hath said, I will dwell in them, and walk in them; and I will be their God, and they shall be my people.*

17.) *Wherefore come out from among them, and be ye separate, saith the Lord, and touch not the unclean thing; and I will receive you,*

18.) *And will be a Father unto you, and ye shall be my sons and daughters, saith the Lord Almighty.*

God truly desires to be a father to you, and he desires for you to be his child. God is not a bad parent. You can trust Him. You can rely on Him. You can believe in him. God is a good parent, even though you may be used to having bad ones. Open your heart once again and let God be a father to you. He'll be the Father you never had, but the Father You'll always need.

Shame in Life #6

Judges 16:1-30

1 Then went Samson to Gaza, and saw there a harlot, and went in unto her. **2** And it was told by the Gazites, saying, Samson is come hither. And they compassed him in, and laid wait for him all night in the gate of the city, and were quiet all the night, saying, In the morning, when it is day, we shall kill him. **3** And Samson lay till midnight, and arose at midnight, and took the doors of the gate of the city, and the two posts, and went away with them, bar and all, and put them upon his shoulders, and carried them up to the top of an hill that is before Hebron. **4** And it came to pass afterward, that he loved a woman in the valley of Sorek, whose name was Delilah. **5** And the lords of the Philistines came up unto her, and said unto her, Entice him, and see wherein his great strength lieth, and by what means we may prevail against him, that we may bind him to afflict him: and we will give thee every one of us eleven hundred pieces of silver. **6** And Delilah said to Samson, Tell me, I pray thee, wherein thy great strength lieth, and wherewith thou mightest be bound to afflict thee. **7** And Samson said unto her, If they bind me with seven green withs that were never dried, then shall I be weak, and be as another man. **8** Then the lords of the Philistines brought up to her seven green withs which had not been dried, and she bound him with them. **9** Now there were men lying in wait, abiding with her in the chamber. And she said unto him, The Philistines be upon thee, Samson. And he brake the withs, as a thread of tow is broken when it toucheth the fire. So his strength was not known. **10** And Delilah said unto Samson, Behold, thou hast mocked me, and told me lies: now tell me, I pray thee, wherewith thou mightest be bound. **11** And he said unto her, If they bind me fast with new ropes that never were occupied, then shall I be weak, and be as another man. **12** Delilah therefore took new ropes, and bound him therewith, and said unto him, The Philistines be upon thee, Samson. And there were leers in wait abiding in the chamber. And he brake them from off his arms like a thread. **13** And Delilah said unto Samson, Hitherto thou hast mocked me, and told me lies: tell me wherewith thou mightest be bound. And he said unto her, if thou weavest the seven locks of my head with the web. **14** And she fastened it with the pin, and said unto him, The Philistines be upon thee, Samson. And he awaked out of his sleep, and went away with the pin of the beam, and with the web. **15** And she said unto him, How canst thou say, I love thee, when thine heart is not with me? thou hast mocked me these three times, and hast not told me wherein thy great strength lieth. **16** And it came to pass, when she pressed him daily with her words, and urged him, so that his soul was vexed unto death; **17** That he told her all his heart, and said unto her, There hath not come a razor upon mine head; for I have been a Nazarite unto God from my mother's womb: if I be shaven, then my strength will go from me, and I shall become weak, and be like any other man. **18** And when Delilah saw that he had told her all his heart, she sent and called for the lords of the Philistines, saying, come up this once, for he hath shewed me all his heart. Then the lords of the Philistines came up unto her, and brought money in their hand. **19** And she made him sleep upon her knees; and she called for a man, and she caused him to shave off the seven locks of his head; and she began to afflict him, and his strength went from him. **20** And she said , The Philistines be upon thee, Samson. And he awoke out of his sleep, and said, I will go out as at other times before, and shake myself. And he wist not that the LORD was departed from him. **21** But the Philistines took him, and put out his eyes, and brought him down to Gaza, and bound him with fetters of brass; and he did grind in the prison house. **22** Howbeit the hair of his head began to grow again after he was shaven. **23** Then the lords of the Philistines gathered them together for to offer a great sacrifice unto Dagon their god, and to rejoice: for they said, Our god hath delivered Samson our enemy into our hand. **24** And when the people saw him, they praised their god: for they said, Our god hath delivered into our hands our enemy, and the destroyer of our country, which slew many of us. **25** And it came to pass, when their hearts were merry, that they said, Call for Samson, that he may make us sport. And they called for Samson out of the prison house; and he made them sport: and they set him between the pillars. **26** And Samson said unto the lad that held him by the hand, suffer me that I may feel the pillars whereupon the house standeth, that I may lean upon them. **27** Now the house was full of men and women; and all the lords of the Philistines were there; and there were upon the roof about three thousand men and women, that beheld while Samson made sport. **28** And Samson called unto the LORD, and said, O Lord GOD, remember me, I pray thee, and strengthen me, I pray thee, only this once, O God, that I may be at once avenged of the Philistines for my two eyes. **29** And Samson took hold of the two middle pillars upon which the house stood, and on which it was borne up, of the one with his right hand, and of the other with his left. **30** And Samson said, let me die with the Philistines. And he bowed himself with all his might; and the house fell upon the lords, and upon all the people that were therein. So the dead which he slew at his death were more than they which he slew in his life.

My shame in life #6 is: "My Weakness." At one time in Samson's life he was married, but there was a big scandal that caused him to lose his wife and she became be married to someone else. Here in chapter 16, he finds himself in love with a prostitute. Sampson was a bravely used by God to help fight Israel's enemies. Simpson was blessed with a super human strength and the power to be a mighty warrior. In one situation, Samson used the jawbone of a donkey's skull as a weapon to fight and kill over 1000 Philistine soldiers. God used his great strength to bring deliverance to the Israelites.

The interesting thing is that Samson falls in love with someone who does not love him. Even though he was the strongest man to ever live, "being a flirt" was the weakness that had him sleeping with a prostitute named; Delilah. Delilah was secretly hired by the Philistine soldiers to find the secret to Samson's power. In verses 6, 10, and 13 Delilah is asking Samson what the secret to his strength is, and every time he gives her an answer she actually tries it to see if it will work. This is also true for some of you. Some of you have areas of your life where you are strong right now, but the problem is the fact that you had been **giving extra attention to your weakness**. Many young people have fallen into their weakness because they believed that they were strong enough not to go that far. Sampson teaches us not to surrender to our weaknesses because it will strip us of our power. The enemy of your soul wants to feed your weakness to steal your power, anointing, testimony and effectiveness.

16.) *And it came to pass, when she pressed him daily with her words, and urged him, so that his soul was vexed unto death;*

17.) *That he told her all his heart...*

Samson was strong but he never dealt properly with his weakness. He never surrounded himself with other strong people. Delilah begged and begged day after day. She pressed and pressed until finally one day Sampson told her the truth about this power. Likewise, the enemy of your soul desires to wear you down to the point that you are too weak to resist. Once you get to this point your weakness will take over your life.

It's like that boyfriend and girlfriend who just start out by holding hands which then turns into holding each other, which becomes kissing and touching. Then it becomes lust and in the heat of the moment you go too far. Temptation always attacks Little by little until one day they add up and become too big to handle. Once this happens, the devil will use your weakness to continually bring shame into your life.

18.) *And when Delilah saw that he had told her all his heart, she sent and called for the lords of the Philistines, saying, Come up this once, for he hath showed me all his heart. Then the lords of the Philistines came up unto her, and brought money in their hand.*

19.) *And she made him sleep upon her knees; and she called for a man, and she caused him to shave off the seven locks of his head; and she began to afflict him, and his strength went from him.*

20.) *And she said, The Philistines be upon thee, Samson. And he awoke out of his sleep, and said, I will go out as at other times before, and shake myself. And he wist not that the LORD was departed from him.*

21.) *But the Philistines took him, and put out his eyes, and brought him down to Gaza, and bound him with fetters of brass; and he did grind in the prison house.*

Samson now tells Delilah that if his hair were to ever be cut it would cause him to lose his strength. Later that evening Samson falls asleep in Delilah's lap, then of course, she cuts his hair. Delilah keeps her agreement with the Philistine soldiers by notifying them when she has discovered the secret to Samson's strength. When the Philistines came to take Samson into custody, Delilah pretended to be concerned. She then awakens the Samson by shouting, "the Philistines are here, defend yourself!"

Samson then jumps up believing that he will defeat the Philistine soldiers just like he had done in times past. The problem is that he did not know his hair had been cut. Samson's power has gone away from him but he does not know it.

Sometimes you can go too far with your weakness. Sexual temptation is not the only weakness that people have. Maybe you are experimenting with things that you shouldn't be touching. Perhaps you have a fascination with something that is ungodly. It could be anything from drugs and drinking to magic and witchcraft. It could be anything like greed or lust or hatred and racism. Maybe it's parties, secular entertainment, or running the streets. These are just areas of weakness in general, but you must identify the weakness in your life. If you do not get the victory over your weaknesses you will live a defeated life as a Christian, unable to maintain the will of God.

22.) *Howbeit the hair of his head began to grow again after he was shaven.*

And now for the good news: maybe you have already fallen into your weakness. Understand that God still has great expectations for your life even though you have made mistakes. Even though Samson had been captured and his head was shaved, his hair began to grow back. As his hair was growing, so was his strength. In verse 18 Samson prayed for God to remember him and strengthen him again.

You need to know that you can recover from your weakness. With the help of the Holy Spirit and stable believers in your life you can regain strength. **Don't let the shame of falling into weakness stop you from growing back stronger.**

When Sampson's strength returned, he was brought out by the Philistines during their time of celebration. They wanted to embarrass and humiliate Samson Further. But as Simpson leaned on the pillars of the building, he was given the strength to push them down causing the building to collapse. The building was so big and so many Philistines were present that when Samson pushed the building down, he killed more Philistines at this one time than he did in all his other battles put together. As you continue to overcome the shame in life, as you continue to gain your strength, you will become a greater threat to the enemy. Take the time to build up your spiritual strength through God's Word, through prayer, fasting, worship, and fellowship with other Christians so that you will be able to bring healing, salvation, peace, and deliverance to others who are also weak.

Chapter 4

"My Habit"

Shame in Life #7

<u>Romans 7:13-21</u>

13 Was then that which is good made death unto me? God forbid. But sin, that it might appear sin, working death in me by that which is good; that sin by the commandment might become exceeding sinful. **14** For we know that the law is spiritual: but I am carnal, sold under sin. **15** For that which I do I allow not: for what I would, that do I not; but what I hate, that do I. **16** If then I do that which I would not, I consent unto the law that it is good. **17** Now then it is no more I that do it but sin that dwelleth in me. **18** For I know that in me (that is, in my flesh,) dwelleth no good thing: for to will is present with me; but how to perform that which is good I find not. **19** For the good that I would I do not: but the evil which I would not, that I do. **20** Now if I do that I would not, it is no more I that do it, but sin that dwelleth in me. **21** I find then a law, that, when I would do good, evil is present with me.

My shame in life #7 is: "My Habit." The apostle Paul allows us to witness his struggle. He is saying that there are good things that he wants to do but he doesn't and finds himself doing evil things which he really does not want to do.

Sometimes in your life there are "things" that you do and you just can't seem to quit. For some reason you keep getting into trouble, into fights, telling lies or cussing. Maybe you find yourself back with worldly friends, or back in the club (even as a Christian). You sincerely want to make changes but continue to find it hard to do.

What is your habit that keeps you from doing what is right? What is the habit that makes you feel dirty inside? Could it be smoking, porn or masturbation? Is it gambling and being deceitful? Maybe it is something not mentioned in this book, but what is mentioned in this book is that your victory for overcoming the shame in life is found in Jesus Christ.

As you have read this book, the Holy Spirit has been showing you areas in your life that you need to deal with. Many subjects have been discussed; many examples have been given. God is ready and willing to give you the help that you need, now you must be willing to honestly open your heart to the Lord and receive this help.

With the Help of the Lord, you can use the following scriptures as a prayer guide:

1 John 1:8-9

8.) If we say that we have no sin, we deceive ourselves, and the truth is not in us.

*9.) If we **confess our sins**, he is faithful and just to forgive us our sins, and to **cleanse us** from all unrighteousness.*

Prayer: Lord I confess that I have sinned. Now I'm asking you to forgive me of my sins. I need you Lord to cleanse my life, cleanse my spirit, and soul from everything that is not right. I can't do it on my own and this is why I give my life to you.

Psalm 51:10-11

10.) *Create in me a **clean heart**, O God; and renew a right spirit within me.*

11.) *Cast me not away from thy presence; and **take not thy holy spirit from me.***

Prayer: Lord, I am asking you to give me a clean heart, give me the right spirit. I don't want to be a stranger to you. Let the Holy Spirit live in me to keep me in your presence.

Galatians 5:1

1.) *Stand fast therefore in the liberty wherewith **Christ hath made us free**, and be not entangled again with the yoke of bondage.*

Prayer: Lord Jesus, I ask you to give me freedom from everything that has brought shame to my life. Free me from the memories of the past, free me from my hurts and disappointments. Keep me from getting tangled up in sinful bondage.

Hebrews 12:1

1.) *Wherefore seeing we also are compassed about with so great a cloud of witnesses, let us **lay aside every weight, and the sin** which doth so easily beset us, and let us run with patience the race that is set before us,*

Prayer: Today I have decided to drop the sin and drop every weight that is too heavy for me so that I can run freely into my destiny. I am letting go of stuff that I've held onto for so long so that I can give the Lord true service and worship.

2 Corinthians 5:17

17.) *Therefore if any man be in Christ, he is a new creature: **old things are passed away;** behold, all things are become new.*

Prayer: Even though I remember the situations of the past, I am letting all the old things die. Lord Jesus, I ask you to reconstruct my life, make me brand-new full of joy and peace.

Romans 8:1

1.) *There is therefore now **no condemnation to them which are in Christ Jesus,** who walk not after the flesh, but after the Spirit.*

There is no more condemnation for me. Jesus has taken away all my shame. I will continue to learn to live a spiritual life and resist more and more the life of the flesh. Thank you, Lord Jesus, for rescuing me from the grip of evil spirits and placing me in the hands of a Loving God!

Chapter 5

"Live without fear or intimidation"

Since you are now in the process of overcoming the shame in life, you must now learn to live for the Lord without Fear or Intimidation. I would like to walk you through 3 points from the book of Daniel that will help you think about how you can continue moving forward from here.

Point #1 - Serve the Lord without fear and intimidation.

<u>Daniel 1:1-8 (KJV)</u>

1.) *In the third year of the reign of Jehoiakim king of Judah came Nebuchadnezzar king of Babylon unto Jerusalem, and besieged it.*

2.) *And the Lord gave Jehoiakim king of Judah into his hand, with part of the vessels of the house of God: which he carried into the land of Shinar to the house of his god; and he brought the vessels into the treasure house of his god.*

3.) *And the king spake unto Ashpenaz the master of his eunuchs, that he should bring certain of the children of Israel, and of the king's seed, and of the princes;*

4.) *Children in whom was no blemish, but well favoured, and skillful in all wisdom, and cunning in knowledge, and understanding science, and such as had ability in them to* *stand in the king's palace, and whom they might teach the learning and the tongue of the Chaldeans.*

5.*) And the king appointed them a daily provision of the king's meat, and of the wine which he drank: so nourishing them three years, that at the end thereof they might stand before the king.*

6.*) Now among these were of the children of Judah, Daniel, Hananiah, Mishael, and Azariah:*

7.*) Unto whom the prince of the eunuchs gave names: for he gave unto Daniel the name of Belteshazzar; and to Hananiah, of Shadrach; and to Mishael, of Meshach; and to Azariah, of Abednego.*

8.*) But Daniel purposed in his heart that he would not defile himself with the portion of the king's meat, nor with the wine which he drank: therefore he requested of the prince of the eunuchs that he might not defile himself.*

We begin by looking into the life of Daniel during the time that the Babylonians have taken over the city of Jerusalem. The Israelites became slaves to Babylon and the king Nebuchadnezzar was a very specific in choosing the type of Israelites to be brought back for his service. Verse 4 tells us that King Nebuchadnezzar wanted those who were skillful and intelligent, and those who were professional and quick learners. Sometimes, however, living in this world there is pressure and temptation. There are worldly things that try to take over our lives in the same way that Babylon took over Jerusalem, because you are just like Daniel. You are gifted, full of talent, full of life and energy.

In verse 5 we see that the king had appointed a specific diet for the slaves to nourish them for his service. In that same way, there are several ways that the devil tries to feed you for the purposes of conditioning you to serve him. He will try feeding you with ungodly friends, secular music and videos, worldly entertainment and movies. In many cases he wants to feed you a false image of who you are so that you will pursue false ideas of what you can become.

While Daniel is under the pressure to obey the king's orders he makes the decision in verse 8, not to defile himself. You must also make the same decision when you are facing the pressures of this world. You must purpose in your heart not to defile yourself.

To defile the means to pollute or contaminate, it means to taint or tarnish. Daniel refused to contaminate himself by living to the king's standards, but rather chose to live pure before God. Daniel was not intimidated by the king, and neither should we be intimidated to have a pure life in the eyes of God. We should not want to live in a way that would cause our spirit, soul, and body to become contaminated with sin and worldliness. Be saved and be proud about it. Be holy and make no excuses for it. Live righteously and know that it is right. We can follow Daniel's example to serve the Lord without fear and intimidation.

Daniel 1:16-20 (KJV)

16.) *Thus Melzar took away the portion of their meat, and the wine that they should drink; and gave them pulse.*

17.) *As for these four children, God gave them knowledge and skill in all learning and wisdom: and Daniel had understanding in all visions and dreams.*

18.) *Now at the end of the days that the king had said he should bring them in, then the prince of the eunuchs brought them in before Nebuchadnezzar.*

19.) *And the king communed with them; and among them all was found none like Daniel, Hananiah, Mishael, and Azariah: therefore stood they before the king.*

20.) *And in all matters of wisdom and understanding, that the king inquired of them, he found them ten times better than all the magicians and astrologers that were in all his realm.*

When Daniel and the three Hebrew boys made the choice to live pure before the Lord, God blessed them in knowledge, skills, learning, wisdom, and for Daniel; visions and dreams. The king was so impressed by these young men that he found them to be 10 times better than his own magicians and astrologers. These young men teach us that living a purified life allows God to make us better. We can excel and rise when we are committed to the Lord. We can accomplish great achievements if we submit our lives to the Lord. If you want to excel and be better in life, live pure unto the Lord.

Point #2 - Worship the Lord without fear and intimidation.

<u>Daniel 3:14-20</u>

14.) *Nebuchadnezzar spake and said unto them, Is it true, O Shadrach, Meshach, and Abednego, do not ye serve my gods, nor worship the golden image which I have set up?*

15.) *Now if ye be ready that at what time ye hear the sound of the cornet, flute, harp, sackbut, psaltery, and dulcimer, and all kinds of music, ye fall down and worship the image which I have made; well: but if ye worship not, ye shall be cast the* *same hour into the midst of a burning fiery furnace; and who is that God that shall deliver you out of my hands?*

16.) Shadrach, Meshach, and Abednego, answered and said to the king, O Nebuchadnezzar, we are not careful to answer thee in this matter.

17.) If it be so, our God whom we serve is able to deliver us from the burning fiery furnace, and he will deliver us out of thine hand, O king.

18.) But if not, be it known unto thee, O king, that we will not serve thy gods, nor worship the golden image which thou hast set up.

19.) Then was Nebuchadnezzar full of fury, and the form of his visage was changed against Shadrach, Meshach, and Abednego: therefore he spake, and commanded that they should heat the furnace one seven times more than it was wont to be heated.

20.) And he commanded the most mighty men that were in his army to bind Shadrach, Meshach, and Abednego, and to cast them into the burning fiery furnace.

    Don't allow anyone to contaminate your worship. This story picks up a significant event in the life of Shadrach, Meshach and Abednego. These were the other three men who chose to stay purified unto God along with Daniel. The Babylonian king has now set up an image of himself as god. People from all around have been gathered for the ceremony of the new golden image and are expected to bow down and worship the image at the sound of the music. Shadrach, Meshach and Abednego have refused to bow down and worship the golden statue.

This is when we pick up on the conversation, in verse 14, when the king asked the young man if it was true that they refused to worship his image. In verse 15 the king offered a second chance for them to bow and worship his image. In verses 16-18 the young man is very specific and direct in letting the king know that no matter what happens they will not serve false gods nor worship his golden image. This response angers king Nebuchadnezzar, which resulted in them being punished by being thrown into a burning furnace of fire.

Don't let anyone intimidate your worship. Sometimes people will want to question why you believe what you believe. Some will question you concerning your faith. Some will question you concerning how you worship. There are even some people who have mixed false teachings into their worship. When you understand that you are worshiping the true and living God through our Lord and Savior Jesus Christ, don't change the way you worship. These three young men would not allow someone who did not know their God to change their mind about their God.

Let's continue to be Daniel chapter 3 verses 24 to 28.

Daniel 3:24-28 (KJV)

*24.) Then Nebuchadnezzar the king was astonied, and rose up in haste, and spake, and said unto his counsellors, **Did not we cast three men bound into the midst of the fire?** They answered and said unto the king, True, O king.*

25.) *He answered and said, Lo,* **<u>I see four men</u>** *loose, walking in the midst of the fire, and they have no hurt;* ***and the form of the fourth is like the Son of God.***

26.) *Then Nebuchadnezzar came near to the mouth of the burning fiery furnace, and spake, and said, Shadrach, Meshach, and Abednego,* ***ye servants of the most high God****, come forth, and come hither. Then Shadrach, Meshach, and Abednego, came forth of the midst of the fire.*

27.) *And the princes, governors, and captains, and the king's counsellors, being gathered together, saw these men, upon whose bodies the <u>fire had no power, nor was an hair of their head singed, neither were their coats changed, nor the smell of fire had passed on them</u>.*

28.) *Then Nebuchadnezzar spake, and said, Blessed be the God of Shadrach, Meshach, and Abednego, who hath sent his angel, and delivered his servants that trusted in him, and have changed the king's word, and yielded their bodies, that they might not serve nor worship any god, except their own God.*

As a result of not bowing down, Shadrach, Meshach and Abednego were thrown into the fiery furnace. As the king was looking into the window of the furnace, we noticed that these three young men were not harmed by the fire. In fact, they were walking around freely without any ropes or chains binding them. The king was fully aware of the fact that there were only three men that were thrown into the fire, but he was astonished to see a <u>fourth man walking with them</u>. The fourth man was described as having the form of the son of God.

It is important to realize how worship creates an atmosphere for the Lord to walk with us. When you live a life of worship, God walks with you in the fire. He walks with you in difficult places and when times are hard. We must never allow ourselves to worship anything or anyone other than the true and living God.

Verse 27 tells us that the fire had no power over these young men. They were not burned, neither did their clothes have the smell of smoke. Worship has a way of keeping the world's fire off of you. Worship as a way of keeping the smell of the world off of you. In other words, a lifestyle of worship protects you from all the influences around you. Even though you may experience walking through many fiery situations, the fire does not have to affect you.

Point #3 - Stand for the Lord without fear and intimidation.

Daniel 6:1-11 (KJV)

1.) It pleased Darius to set over the kingdom an hundred and twenty princes, which should be over the whole kingdom;

2.) And over these three presidents; of whom Daniel was first: that the princes might give accounts unto them, and the king should have no damage.

3.) Then this Daniel was preferred above the presidents and princes, because an excellent spirit was in him; and the king thought to set him over the whole realm.

4.) Then the presidents and princes sought to find occasion against Daniel concerning the kingdom; but they could find none occasion nor fault; forasmuch as he was faithful, neither was there any error or fault found in him.

5.) Then said these men, <u>We shall not find any occasion against this Daniel, except we find it against him concerning the law of his God.</u>

6.) Then these presidents and princes assembled together to the king, and said thus unto him, King Darius, live forever.

7.) All the presidents of the kingdom, the governors, and the princes, the counsellors, and the captains, have consulted together to establish a royal statute, and to make a firm decree, that whosoever shall ask a petition of any God or man for thirty days, save of thee, O king, he shall be cast into the den of lions.

8.) Now, O king, establish the decree, and sign the writing, that it be not changed, according to the law of the Medes and Persians, which altereth not.

9.) Wherefore king Darius signed the writing and the decree.

10.) Now when <u>Daniel knew that the writing was signed</u>, he went into his house; and his windows being open in his chamber toward Jerusalem, he kneeled upon his knees three times a day, and prayed, and gave thanks before his God, as he did aforetime.

11.) Then these men assembled, and found Daniel praying and making supplication before his God.

By this time in the book of Daniel, King Nebuchadnezzar has been driven crazy and loses his throne. Belshazzar became the next king, but he was soon killed. Then we see in this chapter King Darius the median takes over the throne. Verse 1 and 2 says that King Darius was pleased to put Daniel in charge of his kingdom.

Keep in mind that Daniel is a Hebrew, and the other princes and presidents are not. These other leaders knew that Daniel did not serve their false gods, so they searched for a way to get rid of Daniel. Daniel, however, had a spirit of excellence and was very focused on everything that he did. This made it nearly impossible for the other leaders to find any fault in Daniel; therefore, they decided to attack his spiritual beliefs.

These leaders set up a secret meeting with the king to convince him to create a new law. A law that says everyone must pray only to the king for the next 30 days. Even though this meeting was held in secret with the intent of framing Daniel, it was no secret to Daniel. Therefore, he was aware of what the leaders were trying to do to him. Verse 10 tells us that even after Daniel knew this new law was signed and established, he went home and opened his windows and continued to pray to the Lord God like he had always done before.

Daniel teaches us to stand without fear and intimidation. He teaches us to stand for what we believe even when others would want to force us to change our beliefs. Our society puts pressure on Christians not to mention the name Jesus in public, or not to pray to the name of Jesus in public. Some people wish to erase the phrase: *"one nation under God"* from our Pledge of Allegiance. Some people have even succeeded in removing public displays of the 10 Commandments and Nativity scenes during the Christmas holiday. Daniel gives us the courage to stand up for our faith. He gives us the courage to ignore the influence of policies and politics. No matter the pressure we may face in school, at work, or in society, Daniel teaches us to serve the Lord without fear and intimidation.

Chapter 6

"My Testimony"

<u>2 Tim 1:6-12</u>

6 Wherefore I put thee in remembrance that thou stir up the gift of God, which is in thee by the putting on of my hands. **7** For God hath not given us the spirit of fear; but of power, and of love, and of a sound mind. **8** <u>**Be not thou therefore ashamed of the testimony of our Lord**</u>, nor of me his prisoner: but be thou partaker of the afflictions of the gospel according to the power of God; **9** Who hath saved us, and called us with an holy calling, not according to our works, but according to his own purpose and grace, which was given us in Christ Jesus before the world began, **10** But is now made manifest by the appearing of our Savior Jesus Christ, who hath abolished death, and hath brought life and immortality to light through the gospel: **11** Whereunto I am appointed a preacher, and an apostle, and a teacher of the Gentiles. **12** For the which <u>**cause I also suffer these things: nevertheless I am not ashamed**</u>: for I know whom I have believed, and am persuaded that he is able to keep that which I have committed unto him against that day.

<u>Shame in Life #8 "*My Testimony*"</u>

These scriptures give me the power and courage to realize that now that I know I have God's love, God's power, and the ability to have self-control. I **will not be**

ashamed of my testimony. Even though I have been embarrassed and humiliated, I will remember what I have faced in life, and I will tell others how the Lord helped me to overcome. I will tell others how the Lord has saved me and called me according to his own purpose and grace. I am not ashamed because I know the Savior in whom I believe. His name is Jesus and He is the Christ, and I am persuaded that he will keep my life because I have committed my life to him.

Today I will give myself a chance to embrace the new life that Christ gives. I will not live in denial; neither will I pretend that my past never happened. I will not hold on to hatred. I will not be overcome by fear. By using my testimony as a witness of God's goodness, I am able to take away the devil's power of using shame against me.

My life is not controlled by disaster, misfortune, or bad luck. My life is not ruined by abuse, mistakes, and tragedies. I am not responsible for anything that was not in my control. My only responsibility now is to love my Lord and Savior with all my heart, my soul, my mind, and my strength.

Psalm 25:1-3

1.) Unto thee, O LORD, do I lift up my soul.

2.) O my God, I trust in thee: **let me not be ashamed,** *let not mine enemies triumph over me.*

I am overcoming the same in life. I am more than a conqueror. Defeat is not my destiny. I will not forfeit my greatness. I am being restored, revived, and released into a prosperous and productive future.

I will find ways to share my testimony. It could be done in one-on-one conversation, speaking to small groups, posted on blog sites. I may even write a book or an article. Maybe I will even start a Foundation or perhaps God will even direct me into ministry. Jesus endured the greatest form of persecution, abuse, and punishment that anyone could ever receive; but yet his blood and sacrifice was for the purpose of setting me free. It is my prayer and my goal for my life and experiences to become a source of hope, motivation, inspiration, and empowerment to free others who were once like me.

<u>Romans 1:16</u>

16.) For I am not ashamed of the gospel of Christ: for it is the power of God unto salvation to everyone that believeth; to the Jew first, and also to the Greek.

I am not ashamed of the Gospel of Jesus Christ. This Gospel is good news that gives me God's power to be saved. I have been rescued from a path that was leading me into destruction. The good news of Jesus Christ, the power of the Holy Spirit, and the unconditional love of God the Father were the search and rescue team that found me in the worst place of my life. My life has been preserved, daily my mind is being renewed, and I am redeemed.

Those who know me from the past may know me by who <u>I used to be</u> or what <u>I used to do</u>. Family and friends may not understand who I am now. But by the life-changing power of Christ, I am not living in fear or intimidation. I will let my light shine and over time they will see that I have overcome the shame in life.

www.ingramcontent.com/pod-product-compliance
Lightning Source LLC
LaVergne TN
LVHW040202080526
838202LV00042B/3280